M[...] PROGRAM™

Controlling Foodservice Costs
Exam Prep Guide

PEARSON
Prentice
Hall

Upper Saddle River, New Jersey
Columbus, Ohio

NATIONAL
RESTAURANT
ASSOCIATION
S O L U T I O N S ™

DISCLAIMER:

The information presented in this publication is provided for informational purposes only and is not intended to provide legal advice or establish standards of reasonable behavior. Customers who develop food safety-related or operational policies and procedures are urged to obtain the advice and guidance of legal counsel. Although **National Restaurant Association Solutions, LLC (NRA Solutions)** endeavors to include accurate and current information compiled from sources believed to be reliable, **NRA Solutions**, and its **licensor, the National Restaurant Association Educational Foundation (NRAEF)**, distributors, and agents make no representations or warranties as to the accuracy, currency, or completeness of the information. No responsibility is assumed or implied by the NRAEF, NRA Solutions, distributors, or agents for any damage or loss resulting from inaccuracies or omissions or any actions taken or not taken based on the content of this publication.

Sample questions are designed to familiarize the student with format, length and style of the examination questions, and represent only a sampling of topic coverage. The performance level on sample questions does not guarantee passing of a ManageFirst Program examination. Further, the distribution of sample exam questions with their focus on particular areas of subject matter within a ManageFirst Competency Guide is not necessarily reflective of how the questions will be distributed across subject matter on the actual correlating ManageFirst exam.

Visit www.restaurant.org for information on other National Restaurant Association Solutions products and programs.

ManageFirst Program™, ServSafe®, and ServSafe Alcohol® are registered trademarks or trademarks of the National Restaurant Association Educational Foundation, used under license by National Restaurant Association Solutions, LLC a wholly owned subsidiary of the National Restaurant Association.

1 0 9 8 7 6 5 4 3
ISBN-13: 978-0-13-501894-1
ISBN-10:   0-13-501894-3

Contents

How to Take the ManageFirst Examination

The ability to take tests effectively is a learned skill. There are specific things you can do to prepare yourself physically and mentally for an exam. This section helps you prepare and do your best on the ManageFirst Examination.

I. BEFORE THE EXAM

A. How to Study

Study the right material the right way. There is a lot of information and material in each course. How do you know what to study so you are prepared for the exam? This guide highlights what you need to know.

1. **Read the Introduction to each *Competency Guide*.** The beginning section of each guide explains the features and how it is organized.

2. **Look at how each chapter is organized and take clues from the book.**

   - *The text itself is important.* If the text is bold, large, or italicized you can be sure it is a key point that you should understand.

   - *The very first page tells you what you will learn.*

     Inside This Chapter: This tells you at a high level what will be covered in the chapter. Make sure you understand what each section covers. If you have studied the chapter but cannot explain what each section pertains to, you need to review that material.

Learning Objectives: After completing each chapter, you should be able to accomplish the specific goals and demonstrate what you have learned after reading the material. The practice exam as well as the actual exam questions relate to these learning objectives.

- *Quizzes and Tests*

  Test Your Knowledge: This is a pretest found at the beginning of each chapter to see how much you already know. Take this quiz to help you determine which areas you need to study and focus on.

- *Key Terms* are listed at the beginning of each chapter and set in bold the first time they are referred to in the chapter. These terms—new and specific to the topic or ones you are already familiar with—are key to understanding the chapter's content. When reviewing the material, look for the key terms you don't know or understand and review the corresponding paragraph.

- *Exhibits* visually depict key concepts and include charts, tables, photographs, and illustrations. As you review each chapter, find out how well you can explain the concepts illustrated in the exhibits.

- *Additional Exercises*

  Think About It sidebars are designed to provoke further thought and/or discussion and require understanding of the topics.

  Activity boxes are designed to check your understanding of the material and help you apply your knowledge. The activities relate to a learning objective.

- *Summary* reviews all the important concepts in the chapter and helps you retain and master the material.

3. **Attend Review Sessions or Study Groups**. Review sessions, if offered, cover material that will most likely be on the test. If separate review sessions are not offered, make sure you attend class the day before the exam. Usually, the instructor will review the material during this class. If you are a social learner, study with other students; discussing the topics with other students may help your comprehension and retention.

4. **Review the Practice Questions,** which are designed to help you prepare for the exam. Sample questions are designed to familiarize the student with the format, length, and style of the exam questions, and represent only a sampling of topic coverage on the final exam. The performance level on sample questions does not guarantee passing of a ManageFirst Program exam.

B. *How to Prepare Physically and Mentally*

Make sure you are ready to perform your best during the exam. Many students do everything wrong when preparing for an exam. They stay up all night, drink coffee to stay awake, or take sleep aids which leave them groggy and tired on test day.

There are practical things to do to be at your best. If you were an athlete preparing for a major event, what would you do to prepare yourself? You wouldn't want to compete after staying up all night or drinking lots of caffeine. The same holds true when competing with your brain!

1. **Get plenty of sleep.** Lack of sleep makes it difficult to focus and recall information. Some tips to help you get a good night's sleep are:

   - Make sure you have studied adequately enough days before the exam so that you do not need to cram and stay up late the night before the test.
   - Eat a good dinner the night before and a good breakfast the day of the exam.
   - Do not drink alcohol or highly-caffeinated drinks.
   - Exercise during the day, but not within four hours of bedtime.
   - Avoid taking sleep aids.

2. **Identify and control anxiety.** It is important to know the difference between actual test anxiety and anxiety caused by not being prepared.

Test anxiety is an actual physical reaction. If you know the information when you are **not** under pressure but feel physically sick and cannot recall information during the exam, you probably suffer from test anxiety. In this case, you may need to learn relaxation techniques or get some counseling. The key is how you react under pressure.

If you cannot recall information during reviews or the practice exam when you are not under pressure, you have not committed the information to memory and need to study more.

- Make sure you are as prepared as possible. (See "Anxiety Caused by Lack of Preparation")
- Take the exam with a positive attitude.
- Do not talk to other students who may be pessimistic or negative about the exam.
- Know what helps you relax and do it (chewing gum, doodling, breathing exercises).
- Make sure you understand the directions. Ask the instructor questions *before* the test begins.
- The instructor or proctor may only talk to you if you have defective materials or need to go to the restroom. They cannot discuss any questions.
- The instructor or proctor may continuously monitor the students so do not be nervous if they walk around the room.
- Know the skills described in Section II, During the Test.

3. **Anxiety Caused by Lack of Preparation.** The best way to control anxiety due to lack of preparation is focus on the exam. Whenever possible, you should know and do the following:

- Know the location of the exam and how to get there.
- Know if it is a paper-and-pencil test or an online exam. Pencils may be available but bring sufficient number 2 pencils if taking the paper-and-pencil version of the exam.
- If it is an online exam you may need your email address, if you have one, to receive results.
- You are prohibited from using purses, books, papers, pagers, cell phones, or other recording devices during the exam.
- Calculators and scratch paper may be used, if needed. Be sure your calculator is working properly and has fresh batteries.
- The exam is not a timed; however, it is usually completed in less than two hours.
- Take the sample exam so you know what format, style, and content to expect.
- Arrive early so you don't use valuable testing time to unpack.

II. DURING THE TEST

An intent of National Restaurant Association Solutions' ManageFirst exams is to make sure you have met certain learning objectives. If you are physically prepared, have studied the material, and taken the practice exam, you should find the ManageFirst exams to be very valid and fair. Remember, successful test taking is a skill. Understanding the different aspects of test preparation and exam taking will help ensure your best performance.

A. Test Taking Strategies

- Preview the exam for a quick overview of the length and questions.
- Do not leave any question unanswered.
- Answer the questions you are sure of first.

- Stop and check occasionally to make sure you are putting your answer in the correct place on the answer sheet. If you are taking an online exam, you will view one question at a time.
- Do not spend too much time on any one question. If you do not know the answer after reasonable consideration, move on and come back to it later.
- Make note of answers about which you are unsure so you can return to them.
- Review the exam at the end to check your answers and make sure all questions are answered.

B. Strategies for Answering Multiple-Choice Questions

Multiple-choice tests are objective. The correct answer is there, you just need to identify it.

- Try to answer the question before you look at the options.
- Use the process of elimination. Eliminate the answers you know are incorrect.
- Your first response is usually correct.

III. AFTER THE EXAM

Learn from each exam experience so you can do better on the next. If you did not perform on the exam as you expected, determine the reason. Was it due to lack of studying or preparation? Were you unable to control your test anxiety? Were you not focused enough because you were too tired? Identifying the reason allows you to spend more time on that aspect before your next exam. Use the information to improve on your next exam.

If you do not know the reason, you should schedule a meeting with the instructor. As all NRA Solutions ManageFirst exams are consistent, it is important to understand and improve your exam performance. If you cannot identify your problem areas, your errors will most likely be repeated on consecutive exams.

IV. EXAM DAY DETAILS

The information contained in this section will help ensure that you are able to take the exam on the scheduled test day and that you know what to expect and are comfortable about taking the exam.

- Have your photo identification available.
- Anyone with special needs must turn in an *Accommodation Request* to the instructor at least 10 days prior to the exam to receive approval and allow time for preparations. *If needs are not known 10 days prior, you may not be able to take the exam on the scheduled test day.*
- A bilingual English-native language dictionary may be used by anyone who speaks English as a second language. The dictionary will be inspected to make sure there are no notes or extra papers in it.
- If you are ill and must leave the room after the exam has begun you must turn in your materials to the instructor or proctor. If you are able to return, your materials will be returned to you and you may complete the exam. If it is an online exam you must close your browser and if the exam has not been graded yet, login in again when you return.
- Restroom breaks are allowed. Only one person may go at a time and all materials must be turned in prior to leaving the room and picked up when you return; or you must close your browser and login again for online exams.
- Make-up tests may be available if you are unable to take the exam on test day. Check with your instructor for details.
- If you are caught cheating you will not receive a score and must leave the exam location.

Controlling Foodservice Costs Chapter Summaries and Objectives

Chapter 1 What Is Cost Control?

Summary

In most restaurant or foodservice operations, managers take personal charge of an operation's cost control process; however, the size and scope of an operation will determine the extent to which its managers exercise direct control or delegate that responsibility to other staff. If costs get out of line, the profitability of the restaurant could be seriously jeopardized.

At every stage of operations, controls need to be set up to prevent problems and to achieve the goals of the organization. Cost controls start with the menu and continue on through purchasing to receiving, storage, production, and finally, service. Without controls in place, an operation has no way of determining and evaluating whether the operation is profitable or meeting its budget. Controlling and reducing costs are both desirable trends for ensuring the ongoing financial health of an operation.

A standard is a measure that is established to compare levels of attainment for a goal or a measure of adequacy. In the restaurant and foodservice industry, managers, employees, and suppliers are expected to meet the standards set by management. Standards cover the entire spectrum of the restaurant business.

Cost standards vary from one type of operation to another. Costs can be classified in different ways. In the restaurant and foodservice industry, the most common classifications are controllable and noncontrollable costs, as well as fixed, variable, and semivariable costs. The reason for classifying costs is to differentiate between the ones that management can control and those that cannot be controlled. Identifying and understanding these different types of costs help managers interpret cost-related information and make control-related decisions.

Controllable costs are those costs that management can directly control. Noncontrollable costs are those costs over which management has little or no control. Fixed costs are those costs that remain the same regardless of sales volume, while variable costs increase or decrease in direct proportion to increases or decreases in sales volume. Conversely, semivariable costs increase and decrease as sales increase and decrease, but not in direct proportion. Semivariable costs are made up of both fixed costs and variable costs. The two largest costs that management has to control are food cost and labor cost. Together they are known as the prime cost, because these are the two highest costs in the operation.

With experience, managers learn to quickly spot cost-related concerns in their operations. The best way to tell at a glance how an operation is performing is by reading its income statement. Once actual sales and costs are calculated, these figures are monitored and compared to budgeted amounts, operational standards, and historical information in order to identify any variances. When costs are determined to be out of line, the cause should be investigated, and if there is a variance, management should take action to correct the problem causing the variance.

After completing this chapter, you should be able to:
- Describe the relationship between standards and controlling costs.
- Identify the types of costs incurred by a restaurant or foodservice organization.
- Classify foodservice costs as controllable or noncontrollable
- Describe and give examples of controllable and noncontrollable costs.
- Classify foodservice costs as variable, semivariable, or fixed.
- Describe and give example of variable, semivariable, and fixed costs.
- Explain the basic foodservice cost control process.

Chapter 2 A Closer Look at Food Cost

Summary

Many people, including some restaurant or foodservice managers, have a misconception that when food is purchased, it becomes food cost. This is not true. Food cost is the actual dollar value of the food used by an operation during a certain period. It includes the expense to an operation for costs incurred when food is consumed for any reason. Food cost includes the cost of food sold, given away, wasted, or even stolen. Some operations will further refine cost of food sold to get a more accurate number of how all the food is being used.

Fortunately, there is a formula for figuring food cost that takes into account the multiple purchases and uses of food items in a typical restaurant. To determine the value of the food that has been used, you must have both opening and closing inventory data. The formula for calculating food cost starts with adding the opening inventory plus purchases, which is all of the food purchased during that period. The total of these two numbers equals the total food available, or the dollar amount of all food available for sale. The closing inventory is then subtracted from the total food available. This results in the cost of food sold. Most operations inventory and figure food cost monthly, but some quick-service operations conduct inventory on a weekly basis.

Food cost percentage is the relationship between sales and the cost spent on food to achieve those sales. Food cost percentage is often the standard against which food cost is judged. As with any measurement, food cost percentage is most often analyzed by comparing it to company standards, historical costs, or even industry standards. Consistently meeting food cost percentage standards is one of the most difficult tasks for management.

After completing this chapter, you should be able to:
■ Calculate food cost and food cost percentage.
■ Explain the effect that cost and sales have on food cost percentage.

Chapter 3 Using Standardized Recipes to Determine Standard Portion Cost

Summary

In any well-run operation, menu offerings are based on the operation's standards, and staff are expected to meet those standards. If standards are not met, the restaurant will not be profitable. The menu communicates an operation's standards to customers. What is stated on the menu is what the customer expects to get.

The standardized recipe is one of the key tools used in the control process. A standardized recipe is a written format used for consistently preparing and serving a given menu item. It includes a complete list of ingredients, their quantities, and the procedures to be followed each time that recipe is produced. Since a standardized recipe is so important, it must be clearly written and very detailed so that different cooks using the recipe will produce an identical product time after time.

Simply having standardized recipes in an operation is not enough—managers must ensure that all standardized recipes are followed and consistently prepared over time. Any deviation from the standardized recipe results not only in different levels of quality, but also in inaccurate costs being figured for that item and, consequently, an incorrect selling price.

One of the most important reasons for using standardized recipes is to determine how much each serving costs to produce. There are two methods used to determine the cost of ingredients in a standardized recipe. The as purchased (AP) method is used to cost an ingredient at the purchase price prior to any trim or waste being taken into account. The edible portion (EP) method is used to cost an ingredient after it has been trimmed and the waste has been removed to reflect only the usable portion of that item. There is a large difference between these two methods that affects both the quality of the recipe and the costs. It is imperative for a manager to know which method to use when determining the cost of ingredients in a standardized recipe.

Because of cost changes, recipe cost cards should be updated periodically. The reason is, if a cost goes up and the selling price is not adjusted accordingly, the standard food cost percentage will not be met, and the profit of the restaurant will be reduced.

Various computer programs are available for finding the standard cost of a menu item. More and more restaurants, especially the larger ones and the chains, are moving toward automating many of these processes. There are literally scores of software programs available that will produce recipe cost cards.

After completing this chapter, you should be able to:
- Explain why a standardized recipe is important to cost control and product constancy.
- Describe the information included in a standardized recipe.
- Compare "as purchased" and "edible portion" methods of determining the cost of recipe ingredients.
- Develop a recipe cost card using a standardized recipe.

Chapter 4 Cost Control and the Menu—Determining Selling Prices and Product Mix

Summary

The menu, its offerings, and its prices have a large influence on an operation's profit. For a restaurant to be profitable, it must also sell its goods at the correct price from the customers' perspective.

Restaurants use a variety of methods to calculate markup and determine selling prices. The Texas Restaurant Association (TRA) markup method best reflects the direct relationship between profit and selling price. It uses a formula for menu cost markups that takes into account the sales, costs, and profit. The factor method determines menu prices based simply on the standard food cost percentage. The markup on cost method is another formula used to determine a menu selling price based on the standard food cost percentage.

The selling price on the menu is not always the same price that is derived from one of the formulas. Menu selling prices might need to be altered for market-related reasons such as competition, customers' perceptions of the price-value relationship, and markup differentiation.

The menu product mix is a detailed analysis that shows the quantities sold of each menu item, their selling prices, and their standard portion costs. It is used determine the composite food cost percentage for all items sold. It is this average—not each individual item—that must meet the operation's standard food cost percentage.

After completing this chapter, you should be able to:
- Determine a selling price based on various markup methods.
- Explain how market forces affect menu prices.
- Explain how the menu product mix is used to determine the composite food cost of an operation's menu.
- Explain how the menu serves as a food cost control mechanism.

Chapter 5 Controlling Food Costs in Purchasing and Receiving

Summary

Purchasing and receiving are other dimensions in the development of controls in restaurant or foodservice operations. While they are important elements, they are often overlooked in day-to-day operations. Two critical controls are the purchase order and the specification, which tie together the purchasing, receiving, and accounting functions. Other controls include purchasing the correct amount and knowing exactly what is being paid for each item. Calculating AP and EP, as well as conducting butcher tests, gives the buyer the critical information need to make prudent purchases. Knowing when to purchase is also part of a sound purchasing strategy. Perishables, which need to be turned over quickly, must be purchased more often than nonperishable goods. However, even the level of nonperishable goods needs to be sufficient to conduct business, but not so high as to negatively impact cash flow.

The proper receiving procedure includes checking goods against the purchase order and invoice count, weight, and price. The quality of the goods should also be compared to the product specifications to ensure that they meet the operation's standards. Finally, the last step in the process is to put goods away promptly to avoid shrinkage, spoilage, and theft.

After completing this chapter, you should be able to:
- Explain how a specification becomes a control in the purchasing function.
- Explain the parts of a purchase specification and of a purchase order.
- Explain various purchasing methods and their effects on the price of goods.
- Calculate a yield test that identifies the difference between AP price and EP cost.
- Identify factors that affect the purchase price.
- Distinguish between perishable and nonperishable goods and their relationship to the purchasing cycle.
- Calculate the par stock amount to order of a product.
- Calculate the amount to purchase, using EP amount and yield percent.
- Calculate the amount of goods to purchase for catered events.
- Calculate a butcher test, or meat yield test.
- Describe the proper procedures for receiving goods.

Chapter 6 Controlling Food Costs in Storage and Issuing

Summary

Goods in storage are as vulnerable to loss as in any other stage of the process from purchasing to service. The two main causes of loss in storage are spoilage and theft. The storeroom must be kept secure, but not to the point of impeding sales. In addition, goods must be rotated properly, kept at the correct temperature, and turned over frequently to prevent spoilage.

Keeping track of food in storage or inventory is an important part of the control process in restaurant or foodservice operations. Inventory is an operation's control device to help management determine if product that has been received and paid for is actually being used by the kitchen staff and turned into meals that are sold. By knowing the inventory figure, the manager can calculate the cost of food sold, which is management's report card. The cost of food sold tells management if the menu is priced correctly, if the controls in place are working, and how profitable the operation will be. Management also uses cost of food sold to calculate inventory turnover, a control device that tells how fast product in the storeroom is being converted into sales. An additional control point that some operations use is the comparison of physical inventory with perpetual (or theoretical) inventory, which can tell management exactly how much loss is occurring due to spoilage and storage techniques.

Knowing how to prevent and control storage problems and understanding why storage controls are an integral part of the inventory process are vital to the successes of any restaurant or foodservice manager.

After completing this chapter, you should be able to:

- Describe food storage techniques used to control theft.
- Explain the FIFO method of stock rotation.
- Describe the proper method of taking inventory.
- Describe the various methods of inventory pricing.
- Calculate inventory turnover rate and inventory value.
- Compare physical inventory to perpetual inventory, or theoretical inventory.
- Calculate a daily food cost.

Chapter 7 Controlling Food Cost in Production

Summary

One of the primary duties of managing a foodservice facility is to ascertain that the standards of the restaurant are being followed. Two of the primary controls used in production area— standardized recipes and the production chart—were explained in the chapter. Because not adhering to standard recipes is a major cause of increased food cost in production, management's daily ritual should include taste tests of everything on the hot food line and all pantry items in order to confirm adherence to the standard. When a product does not meet the operation's standard, management must immediately determine the reason and take corrective action. In some cases, food can be salvaged; in other cases it must be discarded. While wasting food is serious and will cause an increase in food costs and a decrease in profits, it is much worse to sell a flawed product and lose customers. Regardless of the reason for the food waste, managers must track the waste on the waste report to identify ways to reduce waste and maximize product utilization.

The second cause of increased food cost is preparing the incorrect amount of product. Every operation should strive to product quantities close to the quantity actually needed. If the operation produces too much food, there will be leftovers. Conversely, not producing enough product and running out of an item can disappoint customers and runs the risk that they will not return to the establishment. Either of these scenarios is a lose-lose situation for the restaurant. Many managers use a food production chart to show how much product should be produced by the kitchen for a given meal period. A food production chart is especially useful in foodservice operations where there is a static menu.

Although the food production report states the appropriate amount to produce, some recipes do not yield the needed amount. Managers use two tools to ensure that produced quantity is in line with the food production chart. One tool is recipe conversion, which allows management or food production personnel to change a recipe's original yield to the desired yield. This formula ensures that all of a recipe's ingredients stay in the proper proportion. Occasionally, a recipe does not yield the expected number of portions. In this case, management uses a second tool, recipe yield process, to determine the number of portions that a recipe will produce. Depending on how the portion size is stated, the total volume of the recipe is calculated either by weight or by volume.

Diligently using the controls and tools explained in this chapter will enable you to keep your establishment's food costs in line with your standards.

After completing this chapter, you should be able to:
- Develop a food production chart.
- Describe how a waste report helps control food costs.
- Use a conversion factor to calculate a new yield for an existing recipe.
- Determine a recipe's yield and the number of portions it will produce.

Chapter 8   Controlling Food Cost in Service and Sales

Summary

Management must be extremely vigilant in the service area to control food cost. Two of the greatest threats are overportioning and theft of cash. Every item served, no matter how small, should have a correct portion assigned to it by management. This chapter reviewed the various portion control devices that can be utilized to ensure that portion-size standards are met. The chapter also discussed the importance of supervising employees to ensure correct portioning, and the importance of continuous training and follow-through, which can increase the success of your control process.

A variety of reports, such as the waste report, cash report, and daily sales report, can help management pinpoint areas in need of additional cost control. These reports can also aid management in finding the root cause of cost control problems within the organization.

Two different methods of controlling cash in sales were described. One is a manual system of duplicate guest checks, while the other is a POS control system that involves the use of technology. More and more operations are moving toward the use of automated computer systems to manage this area of sales. However, management must remember that simply adding technology to the process will not ensure a good control system. Such a system must be designed effectively and used properly by managers and staff.

In addition, a cash control system must be in place in all operations. As part of this process, servers should be responsible for their assigned checks and for monies collected. Various cash handling procedures can be used, depending on the operation. When the time comes to check the daily sales, two or more staff members should be responsible for checking it against the daily receipts. Given the threat of theft in the cash handling process, this area of the operation should be supervised more closely than others.

After completing this chapter, you should be able to:
- Explain the importance of portion control to food cost.
- Describe various portion control devices and their uses.
- Explain the importance of training, monitoring, and follow-through in portion control.
- Compare the duplicate guest-check system to the POS control system for controlling the receipt of money.
- List the benefits of each payment method used by the restaurant and foodservice industry.
- Describe cash handling procedures used in operations.
- Complete a daily sales report.

Chapter 9 Controlling Labor Costs

Summary

This chapter introduced the elements that help management control labor cost. Labor cost includes, in addition to payroll cost, such costs as the employer's contribution to FICA and Medicare, workers' compensation insurance, and employee benefits. Although total labor cost might be a large number, management is most concerned about the relationship between labor cost and sales. By looking at labor cost as a percentage, the relationship between labor cost and sales is taken into account. With labor being one of the highest costs for which management is responsible, it is imperative that management uses every tool available to control this cost.

One control management uses to keep labor cost in control is the budget. Having a budget helps mangers plan the financial activities related to their daily operations. For an operation to achieve its budgeted profit, the sales projections listed in its budget must be met. Additionally, the operation's costs must be held to their standards. Accurate historical sales information and projected sales are vitally important to an accurate budget. Budget accuracy is important because the budget is the foundation on which management builds the master schedule.

The primary control for managing labor cost is the schedule. Once you know the dollars available for labor scheduling, you can begin to create a schedule. The right number of people with the right combination of experience and productivity levels must be available to work each shift. If too many people are scheduled, labor costs increase. Conversely, if too few people are scheduled, service may be poor and result in a loss of sales. Restaurant and foodservice managers often use a master schedule to simplify the preparation of weekly schedules. There is little margin for error when planning a schedule so that it meets the labor cost standard and still allows for the appropriate number of staff to provide good service.

While scheduling has a direct effect on labor cost on a day-today basis, there are other factors that directly influence it, including employee turnover, employee benefits, and labor contracts. Quality and productivity standards affect labor cost indirectly. Management can use sales per person-hour, covers per person-hour, and sales per cover to monitor productivity and to spot problems before they cause an increase in labor cost.

After completing this chapter, you should be able to:
- Distinguish between fixed, variable, and semivariable costs.
- Explain how payroll cost, FICA, Medicare, and employee benefits make up labor cost.
- Describe the components and factors to consider in the development of a master schedule.
- Explain the difference between a master schedule and a crew schedule.
- List factors that affect labor cost.
- Explain how direct factors, such as business volume, affect labor cost.
- Calculate turnover rate percentage, total dollars for labor costs, dollars available for scheduling, and hours available for scheduling.
- Explain how indirect factors, such as quality and productivity standards, affect labor costs.

Controlling Foodservice Costs Practice Questions

Please note the numbers in parentheses following each question. They represent the chapter and page number, respectively, where the content in found in the ManageFirst Competency Guide.

IMPORTANT: These sample questions are designed to familiarize the student with format, length and style of the examination questions, and represent only a sampling of topic coverage.

The grid below represents how the *actual* exam questions will be divided across content areas on the corresponding ManageFirst Program exam.

Controlling	1.	What Is Cost Control?	10
Foodservice	2.	A Closer Look at Food Cost	11
Costs	3.	Using Standardized Recipes to Determine Standard Portion Cost	9
	4.	Cost Control and the Menu—Determining Selling Prices and Product Mix	10
	5.	Controlling Foodservice Costs in Purchasing and Receiving	9
	6.	Controlling Food Cost in Storage and Issuing	6
	7.	Controlling Food Cost in Production	8
	8.	Controlling Food Cost in Service and Sales	9
	9.	Controlling Labor Costs	8
		Total No. of Questions	**80**

The performance level on sample questions does not guarantee passing of a ManageFirst Program examination. Further, the distribution of sample exam questions with their focus on particular areas of subject matter within a ManageFirst Competency Guide is not necessarily reflective of how the questions will be distributed across subject matter on the actual correlating ManageFirst exam.

1. When the cost of the ingredients went up, the manager changed a standard recipe to reduce the portion size. This change is an example of what type of action to control food costs? (1, 13)
   A. Corrective
   B. Profit
   C. Margin
   D. Menu

2. An item that weighs 8 pounds as purchased yields 4 pounds. The restaurant needs 50 pounds of edible portions until the next time the supplier delivers. How many pounds should the buyer order? (5, 76)
   A. 25 pound
   B. 50 pounds
   C. 100 pounds
   D. 200 pounds

3. According to the Competency Guide, in addition to the POS control system, what is the other widely used method used to track customer orders for menu items? (8, 138)
   A. Duplicate guest check
   B. Signed invoice
   C. Charge card receipt
   D. Verbal order from the server.

4. What role does the recipe cost card play in an operation? (3, 33)
   A. It is a rule of thumb for the cooks to follow when preparing a specific menu item.
   B. It is a tool to calculate the standard portion cost for a menu item.
   C. It is a listing of ingredients and cooking instructions for a menu item.
   D. It is a list of inventory costs of ingredients for a particular menu item.

5. When reviewing the weekly waste report, the manager notices many food items were discarded for the following reasons: burnt, spoiled, made incorrectly, and left out of the cooler too long before serving. What are the two most likely causes of repeated food waste? (7, 116)
   A. No stock rotation and sub–par stock levels
   B. The cooks' and the servers' poor performance
   C. Poor training for staff and lack attention by management
   D. Errors in the food production chart and the standard recipe cards

6. The recipe for tamales calls for 8 ounces of corn meal. Corn meal has an as purchased (AP) cost of $30.00 for a 20-pound bag. What is the standard portion cost of the cornmeal that is on the recipe cost card? (3, 33-35)
   A. $0.37
   B. $0.50
   C. $0.75
   D. $1.00

7. What is a standard? (1, 3)
   A. A measure that is established to determine levels of attainment for a goal
   B. An item to exchange for a benefit or goal
   C. A series of steps to achieve a goal
   D. A defined quantity that is used to count things

8. What is portion size, item placement, eye appeal, and garnish considered when referring to appearance of a menu item when served? (8, 135)
   A. Recipe preparation
   B. Plate presentation
   C. Ingredient compilation
   D. Value proposition

9. If projected sales for the first week of November are $75,000 and the standard labor cost percentage is 33 percent, what are the total dollars available for labor? (9, 160)
   A. $25,000
   B. $50,000
   C. $225,000
   D. Not enough information is given

10. The delivery of a food order arrives and sits for a few hours until the chef has time to store the goods. What is the result of this poor receiving procedure? (5, 83)
    A. The quality of the meat and produce is very good.
    B. Food costs are higher than they should be.
    C. The content of the order is checked to verify no shortages in the delivery.
    D. Theft is prevented by focusing on the cash register instead.

11. A food production chart is the best way to (7, 113)
    A. reuse leftover food servings for the next day's entree.
    B. offer a different menu every day.
    C. know how much food to produce during a given meal period.
    D. know how big the supply of the ingredients is in the storeroom.

12. How can nonperishable goods be best described? (5, 73)
    A. These products have an indefinite shelf life.
    B. These products should be purchased as often as possible.
    C. These items can only be purchased from one supplier.
    D. These products that have a relatively short shelf life.

13. The manager uses the following figures to calculate the menu selling price of a peking chicken dinner: labor expense is 33%, other expenses are 20%, profit is budgeted at 10% of sales, and the standard portion cost is $3.70. What menu price should the manager set for a peking chicken dinner, using the Texas Restaurant Association method to determine prices? (4, 44)
    A. $4.07
    B. $6.03
    C. $10.00
    D. $37.00

14. What is the formula to calculate gross profit? (1, 11)
    A. Subtract the total expenses of the entire restaurant operation from the total revenues.
    B. Add the ingredients for all the menu items.
    C. Subtract the cost of food from the sales.
    D. Compare the actual food costs with the food cost percentage times the sales.

15. The daily production chart calls for 15 portions of crab bisque. The crab bisque recipe is for 20 portions. What is the recipe conversion factor? (7, 118)
    A. −5
    B. 0.25
    C. 0.75
    D. 1.33

16. The standard portion size of meatloaf is 12 ounces of hamburger that costs $1.20 and sells for $4.99. If the kitchen mistakenly used 14 ounces of hamburger instead, what happens to the food cost percentage? (2, 23-24)
    A. It goes up from 24% to 28%.
    B. It goes down from 28% to 24%.
    C. It is the same because the selling price is still $4.99.
    D. It changes from 10 cents to 13 cents per serving.

17. According to the Competency Guide, what is a common tool used for portion control of sauces and soups? (8, 133)
    A. Slotted serving spoon
    B. Portion control scale
    C. POS system
    D. Ladle

18. A manager promised the owner to reduce the turnover rate from 200% to 150% per year. If the restaurant has 160 employees on average per year and a new hire costs an average of $500 to recruit, hire and train, how much money will the manager save the restaurant owner with the lower turnover rate? (9, 170)
    A. $4,000
    B. $40,000
    C. $80,000
    D. Not enough information is given

19. The manager discovers the spaghetti sauce tastes very salty during the daily taste test and does not meet standard. Upon investigation, it looks as if the cook accidentally used salt instead of sugar in the recipe. What should be done with the spaghetti sauce? (7, 111-112)
    A. Use the spaghetti sauce anyway, as guests will not know the difference.
    B. Ask someone else to taste the sauce using the same spoon.
    C. Sell the sauce, but make sure every server tells each guest that the spaghetti sauce is a special recipe today.
    D. Discard the spaghetti sauce because it will not likely taste to standard.

20. Insurance is an example of what kind of cost? (1, 5)
    A. Controllable
    B. Prime
    C. Noncontrollable
    D. Semivariable

21. Based on sales history and the weather, the management expects to serve 70 meals today at lunch. The lunch menu is expected to sell in these proportions: tuna salad sandwich, 20%; chicken caesar salad, 25%; fried chicken lunch, 30%; meatloaf, 15%; and pastrami and kraut, 10%. How many portions of pastrami and kraut should be prepared for the lunch interval? (7, 113-114)
    A. 7
    B. 14
    C. 18
    D. 21

22. Management is comparing the productivity of servers who work the weekend dinner shifts. Over the past two weeks, Kim worked 12 hours and had sales of $1,200. Roberto worked 18 hours with sales of $2,100. Jamal worked 16 hours with sales of $2,100, and Melee worked 10 hours with sales of $1,200. Which server had the best productivity measured by sales per hour? (9, 175)
    A. Kim
    B. Roberto
    C. Jamal
    D. Melee

23. A manager checked the inventory and found that there are three bushels of apples on hand with a cost of $20.00 per bushel, four gallons of milk on hand with a cost of $2.00 per gallon, and ½ case of peanut oil with a cost of $35.00 per case. What is the extended cost of inventory on hand? (6, 99)
    A. $85.50
    B. $103.50
    C. $123.00
    D. $156.00

24. Prime costs are the two largest expenses that the management team has to control. What do these two expenses include? (1, 9)
    A. Inventory cost and spoilage cost
    B. Taxes and social security payments
    C. Food cost and labor cost
    D. Rent and licensing fees

25. Name the three details of all menu items a menu product mix analysis looks at. (4, 49)
    A. Markup differentiations, menu item categories, customer expectations
    B. Popularities, profitability, variances
    C. Recipe ingredients, serving portions, cooking instructions
    D. Quantities sold, standard portion costs, selling prices

26. If the budgeted food cost is 25%, the sales for the month of July are $100,000, and the actual food cost was $30,000, what is the variance? (1, 11)
    A. 5%
    B. 25%
    C. $5,000
    D. $25,000

27. The manager has set a par stock level of 18 cases for French fries. The buyer does the inventory and counts 10 cases on hand. How many cases should be ordered? (5, 75)
    A. 2 cases
    B. 8 cases
    C. 18 cases
    D. 28 cases

28. If the forecasted dollars available for labor equal $68,000, benefit costs equal $12,600, and manager salaries equal $26,400, what are the dollars available for variable-cost employees? (8, 161)
    A. $20,000
    B. $29,000
    C. $31,600
    D. $55,400

29. What includes details about ingredients, quantities, instructions, and portion sizes? (3, 29)
    A. Standardized recipes
    B. Inventories
    C. Food costs
    D. Corrective actions

30. If the actual week's food cost is $1,000 and the food cost percentage is 25%, what are the actual sales for that week? (2, 22)
    A. $250
    B. $1,000
    C. $4,000
    D. $12,000

31. The manager determines that the September opening inventory was $15,000, the closing inventory was $11,000, and the cost of food sold was $65,000. What was the inventory turnover rate for September? (6, 102-103)
    A. 0.2
    B. 2.5
    C. 5.0
    D. 7.0

32. What does the as purchased (AP) portion method of costing ingredients mean? (3, 31)
    A. Only the usable amount of the ingredients is costed.
    B. Only the portion of the ingredients that tastes good is costed.
    C. The ingredients are costed in the form in which they are purchased.
    D. The costed ingredients have waste and shrinkage subtracted.

33. Available cost increases in direct proportion to what? (1, 7)
    A. Inventory
    B. Labor
    C. Profits
    D. Sales

34. Large foodservice units such as schools, hospitals, or the government typically use which purchasing method? (5, 68)
    A. Standing order
    B. Cost-plus
    C. Sealed bids
    D. Commissary

35. According to the Competency Guide, the schedule is the primary control tool for managing what? (9, 167)
    A. Noncontrollable costs
    B. Fixed costs
    C. Labor costs
    D. Staff discipline

36. If a crab cake dinner sells for $20.00 and the food cost is $5.60, what is the food cost percentage? (2, 22)
   A. 22%
   B. 25%
   C. 28%
   D. 30%

37. A restaurant has negotiated a lease for $1,500 per month plus 2% of the monthly gross sales. What type of cost is this lease? (1, 7)
   A. Fixed
   B. Semivariable
   C. Variable
   D. Controllable

38. What is an example of good food storage inventory security (eg. inventory security)? (6, 93)
   A. Establishing a par stock for the start of each shift
   B. Keeping stock close to the staff that uses it
   C. Conducting an inventory
   D. Keeping fewer items in storage

39. According to the Competency Guide, menu engineering is the process of analyzing the menu product mix plus what? (4, 50)
   A. The contribution margins and the menu items' popularity
   B. The price-value relationship and the competitors' menus
   C. The markup differentiations and the menu item categories
   D. The menu items markups and the labor to prepare menu items

40. Sales for January were $35,000 and the food cost percentage was 40%. What was the actual food cost in dollars for January? (2, 22)
   A. $1,400
   B. $8,750
   C. $14,000
   D. $21,000

41. When preparing sales projections for the following week, the manager gathers the following information: sales for the Saturday meal period were $250 three weeks ago, $275 two weeks ago, and $300 last week. What would the manager likely use to base the schedule on for next Saturday? (8, 159)
  A. $150
  B. $200
  C. $300
  D. $375

42. Food purchases in July totaled $27,200. Inventory on hand July 1 was $18,000 and inventory on hand July 31 was $10,500. What was the cost of food sold in July? (2, 20)
  A. $1,300
  B. $27,200
  C. $34,700
  D. $55,700

43. The chef directs the kitchen staff to weigh 25 four-ounce servings of sliced turkey breast, place each serving in individual baggies, and put them into the cooler on the line. What is the advantage of this preportioning effort to the business? (8, 132)
  A. The staff can work more paid hours.
  B. The staff can perform the portion control more efficiently and accurately.
  C. The staff can have a break while the food is prepared for each order.
  D. The staff has fewer tasks from the manager.

44. Labor costs are the sum of which two categories of costs? (9, 154)
  A. Insurance and taxes
  B. Wages and salaries
  C. Fixed and semivariable costs
  D. Payroll and employee benefits

45. What does First in/first out (FIFO) for stock rotation mean? (6, 89)
  A. The oldest items are used first.
  B. The oldest items are used last.
  C. The newest items are used first.
  D. The items are dated for the staff.

46. The standard crab bisque recipe includes 12 ounces of crab meat, ½ gallon of whole milk, 1.5 liters of dry sherry, 16 ounces of light cream, 2 tablespoons of salt, and 1 teaspoon black pepper. Using a conversion factor of 1.2 percent calculate how much crab meat to use. (7, 118)
    A. 10 ounces
    B. 13.2 ounces
    C. 14.4 ounces
    D. 19.2 ounces

47. What would a manager use to set the restaurant's policy to use only Chinook salmon from Alaska in the chef's special offering for next week? (5, 63)
    A. Invoice
    B. Standard recipe
    C. Par stock
    D. Specification

48. The restaurant plans to serve a banquet for 500 guests. Two hundred guests chose fish and three hundred guests chose chicken. The edible portion yield is 50% for 10 ounces per serving of fish and 75% for 8 ounces per serving of chicken. How much fish and how much chicken should the buyer order? (5, 77)
    A. 125 pounds of fish and 175 pounds of chicken
    B. 100 pounds of fish and 400 pounds of chicken
    C. 200 pounds of fish and 150 pounds of chicken
    D. 150 pounds of fish and 200 pounds of chicken

49. The formula for calculating food cost is opening inventory _____ purchases _____ closing inventory. (2, 22)
    A. plus, minus
    A. plus, plus
    B. minus, plus
    C. minus, minus

50. Why does a manager use a physical inventory? (6, 104)
    A. To track the bar supplies separately from the kitchen supplies
    B. To track the supplies for the entire restaurant operation
    C. To avoid spoilage
    D. To estimate the daily food cost percentage

Controlling Foodservice Costs
Answer Key to Practice Questions

1. A	26.C
2. C	27.B
3. A	28.B
4. B	29.A
5. C	30.C
6. C	31.C
7. A	32.C
8. B	33.D
9. A	34.C
10.B	35.C
11.C	36.C
12.A	37.B
13.C	38.A
14.C	39.A
15.C	40.C
16.A	41.C
17.D	42.C
18.B	43.B
19.D	44.D
20.C	45.A
21.A	46.C
22.C	47.D
23.A	48.D
24.C	49.A
25.D	50.B

Controlling Foodservice Costs Explanations to the Answers for the Practice Questions

Question #1
Answer A is correct. The manager maintained the standard food cost percentage with a corrective action.

Answer B is wrong. The food costs are only one of many factors in the profits of the restaurant.

Answer C is wrong. The food costs are only one of many factors in the margins of the restaurant.

Answer D is wrong. The menu was not changed unless the portion size was listed on the menu. The example does not have this menu detail.

Question #2
Answer A is wrong. The buyer does NOT multiply (error) by the yield percentage of 50%. The buyer should have divided by 50%.

Answer B is wrong. The buyer has to take into account the waste by using the yield percentage.

Answer C is correct. The calculation is as follows:
1. $4 \div 8 = 50\%$ yield percentage.
2. 50 lbs $\div 50\% = 100$ pounds to purchase.

Answer D is wrong. 4 lb EP $\times$ 50 lb = 200 lbs (error) does NOT use the yield percentage in the calculation

Question #3
Answer A is correct. The duplicate guest check records the menu items the guests ordered.

Answer B is wrong. An invoice is a signed agreement that contains the goods and the price paid. Normally the customer does NOT sign an order. The duplicate guest check can serve as an equivalent to an unsigned invoice, but this usage is NOT a common practice in the restaurant industry.

Answer C is wrong. The charge card receipt does NOT track what was ordered, only what was paid.

Answer D is wrong. A verbal order does NOT provide a permanent record to track the order.

Question #4

Answer A is wrong. A well managed restaurant has formally documented standard recipe cards and recipe cost cards for all items on the menu. A rule of thumb is NOT sufficient.

Answer B is correct. The recipe cost card is use for portion cost control.

Answer C is wrong. This answer describes a standard recipe card, NOT a recipe cost card. The recipe cost card has cost information for each of the ingredients.

Answer D is wrong. The inventory costs are the value of food in storage and do NOT contain cost information for a particular menu item.

Question #5

Answer A is wrong. Lack of stock rotation may increase waste due to spoilage. However, shortages below par stock level do NOT result in waste, but in lost sales.

Answer B is wrong. Poor performance can cause repeated food waste. However poor performance for the entire staff is an indication of poor training.

Answer C is correct. Causes of food waste are usually poor training and lack of attention.

Answer D is wrong. Errors in the food production chart and the standard recipe cards can be fixed once, so they cannot be the cause of repeated food waste.

Question #6

Answer A is wrong. See Answer C.

Answer B is wrong. See Answer C.

Answer C is correct. The calculation is as follows:

1. The number of ounces in a bag of cornmeal is 800 ounces. 20 pounds per bag × 16 ounces per pound = 320 ounces per bag.
2. The number of servings in a bag of cornmeal is 40 servings. 320 ounces per bag ÷ 8 ounces per serving = 40 servings per bag.
3. The per-standard cost of the cornmeal per serving is $0.75 $30.00 per bag ÷ 40 servings per bag = $0.75 per serving.

Answer D is wrong. See Answer C.

Question #7

Answer A is correct. A standard is the measure that a business establishes to compare levels of attainment towards a goal.
Answer B is wrong. A cost is something, such as time or money, exchanged for a benefit or a goal.
Answer C is wrong. A procedure is a series of steps to achieve a goal.
Answer D is wrong. A unit of measure is a precisely defined quantity, such as dollars or pounds, to count things.

Question #8

Answer A is wrong. Preparation includes selecting ingredients, measuring, mixing, and cooking. The plate presentation is the last step in preparation before the item is served to the guest.
Answer B is correct. Appearance of the menu item as served to the guest is the plate presentation.
Answer C is wrong. The ingredients are the first step in preparation. Plate presentation is the last step in preparation.
Answer D is wrong. The value is the customer's perception of the menu item. Plate presentation enhances the customer's dining experience. Customers "eat with their eyes."

Question #9

Answer A is correct. The calculation is as follows:
$$\$75,000 \times 0.33 = \$25,000$$
Answer B is wrong. The calculation does not use the remainder percentage.
$$\$75,000 \times (1 - 0.33 = 0.66) \text{ (error)} = \$50,000.$$
Answer C is wrong. The calculation uses the percentage to multiply; NOT divide.
$$\$75,000 \div \text{(error)} \ 0.33 = \$225,000$$
Answer D is wrong. There is sufficient information to calculate the total dollars available for labor.

Question #10

Answer A is wrong. The quality can only be worse, resulting in unnecessary waste that contributes directly into increased costs.

Answer B is correct. Poor receiving practices can result in higher food costs, due to spoilage, shortages or theft.

Answer C is wrong. The order may never get reconciled, resulting in shortages that mean increased costs.

Answer D is wrong. Theft of delivered items is invited with poor receiving procedures, which means increased costs.

Question #11

Answer A is wrong. Use of leftovers should be avoided because their taste and appearance may NOT be suitable for customers.

Answer B is wrong. A food chart is not useful without a history of prior sales.

Answer C is correct. A food chart shows how much food should be prepared for a given period of time when the menu is stable.

Answer D is wrong. The food production chart does NOT track the ingredients from the storeroom to the kitchen.

Question #12

Answer A is correct. Nonperishable goods have a relatively long shelf life.

Answer B is wrong. Nonperishable good should be purchased as seldom as possible due to the impact of the size of the storage area, the operation's cash flow, and location.

Answer C is wrong. The purchase method does NOT impact the shelf life of the goods.

Answer D is wrong. Perishable goods have a relatively short shelf life, NOT a long shelf life.

Question #13
Answer A is wrong. $3.70 + (10% of $3.70 (error) = $0.37) = $4.07.
This answer adds 10% of the portion cost to the portion cost in error.
The TRA method is NOT a markup calculation.
Answer B is wrong. $3.70 ÷ 0.63 = $6.03 (error).
This answer missed a step in the TRA method: calculating the divisor.
Answer C is correct. The menu price is calculated with the TRA
method as follows:
1. Add the expenses as decimal percentages
   0.33 + 0.20 + 0.10 = 0.63
2. Subtract the total expenses percentage from 1.00 to get the
   divisor.
   1.00 − 0.63 = 0.37. [Note: 37% is the food cost percentage for
   this menu item.]
3. Divide the standard portion cost by the divisor.
   $3.70 ÷ 0.37 = $10.00.
Answer D is wrong. $3.70 ÷ 0.10 (error) = $37.00
The divisor in the TRA method does NOT use the profit percentage
alone; it must use all expense percentages.

Question #14
Answer A is wrong. This calculation is the net profits.
Answer B is wrong. The gross profit is measured in dollars not
ingredients.
Answer C is correct. The gross profit is the amount of money made
on the cost of food sold.
Answer D is wrong. This calculation is the food-cost variance.

Question #15

Answer A is wrong. The calculation is a division, NOT a subtraction. The conversion factor is never a negative number.

$$15 - 20 = -5 \text{ (error)}$$

Answer B is wrong. The calculation does not subtract from 1. The following calculation is wrong:

$$1.00 - (15 \div 20 = 0.75) = 0.25 \text{ (error)}$$

Answer C is correct. The conversion factor is 0.75. The calculation is as follows:

$$15 \text{ portions} \div 20 \text{ portions} = 0.75$$

Answer D is wrong. The conversion factor is the (desired yield) ÷ (recipe yield). This calculation reversed the numbers as follows:

$$20 \div 15 = 1.25 \text{ (error)}$$

Question #16

Answer A is correct. The food cost percentage goes up. The original food cost percentage is calculated as $1.20 ÷ $5.00 = 24%. The mistaken quantity is calculated as follows: the cost of hamburger is $1.20 ÷ 12 ounces = $0.10 per ounce; 14 ounces costs $1.40 per serving; the mistaken food cost percentage is $1.40 ÷ $5.00 = 28%.
Answer B is wrong. The food cost went up so the food cost percentage CANNOT go down.
Answer C is wrong. The food cost went up and so the food cost percentage has to go up too even though the selling price stayed the same.
Answer D is wrong. This answer is in terms of actual food costs per serving; NOT food cost percentage. Food cost percentage is expressed independently from the size of the portions to make comparisons easier to manage.

Question #17

Answer A is wrong. A slotted spoon is used to serve solid food portions without the liquids used in preparation.
Answer B is wrong. A scale is used to control serving portions by weight.
Answer C is wrong. POS is a point of sale system that is NOT used for portion control.
Answer D is correct. A ladle is used to control serving portions of sauces and soups.

Question #18

Answer A is wrong. There is an arithmetic error in steps 3 and 6.

1. $200\% \div 100 = 2.0$
2. 160 average number of employees $\times$ 2.0 turnover per year = 320 new employees per year
3. 320 new employees $\times$ \$500 per new employee = \$16,000 (error)
4. $100\% \div 100 = 1.0$
5. 160 average number of employees $\times$ 1.5 turnover per year = 240 new employees per year
6. 240 new employees $\times$ \$500 per new employee = \$12,000 (error)
7. $\$16,000 - \$12,000 = \$4,000$.

Answer B is correct. The calculation is as follows:

1. The current turnover is 2.0
   $200\% \div 100 = 2.0$
2. The current number of new employees per year is 320.
   160 average number of employees $\times$ 2.0 turnover per year = 320 new employees per year
3. The total annual cost for training new employees is \$160,000
   320 new employees $\times$ \$500 per new employee = \$160,000
4. The promised turnover is 1.5
   $100\% \div 100 = 1.0$
5. The promised number of new employees per year is 160.
   160 average number of employees $\times$ 1.5 turnover per year = 240 new employees per year
6. The total annual cost for training new employees is \$120,000
   240 new employees $\times$ \$500 per new employee = \$120,000
7. The promised savings is \$40,000
   $\$160,000 - \$120,000 = \$40,000$.

Answer C is wrong. There is an error in step 4 that used the wrong turnover.
1. $200\% \div 100 = 2.0$
2. 160 average number of employees $\times$ 2.0 turnover per year = 320 new employees per year
3. 320 new employees $\times$ $500 per new employee = $160,000
4. 100% (error) $\div$ 100 = 1.0
5. 160 average number of employees $\times$ 1.0 turnover per year = 160 new employees per year
6. 160 new employees $\times$ $500 per new employee = $80,000
7. $160,000 - $80,000 = $80,000.

Answer D is wrong. There is sufficient information in the question to get an answer.

Question #19
Answer A is wrong. Guests may not know there was a mistake, but they can recognize that the quality is not to their expectations. Inferior product jeopardizes future business.

Answer B is wrong. While asking for another opinion is ok, using the same spoon is not practicing good sanitation.

Answer C is wrong. The standard recipe is the main quality control. The manager has to approve changes to the standard recipe before serving to customers.

Answer D is correct. When a product cannot be fixed, then it must be discarded. By discarding the spaghetti sauce, the food cost goes up and profits go down. While wasting food is serious, it is worse to serve inferior product and lose customers.

Question #20
Answer A is wrong. Insurance costs are not controllable after the policy has been negotiated.

Answer B is wrong. Prime costs include food costs and labor costs.

Answer C is correct. Management cannot control the insurance costs after the policy has been negotiated.

Answer D is wrong. Insurance costs are fixed costs in relation to sales volume.

Question #21
Answer A is correct. The kitchen should prepare enough to have 7 servings of pastrami and kraut. The calculation is 10% of 70 = 7 servings.
Answer B is wrong. The kitchen should NOT prepare enough to have 14 servings of pastrami and kraut. The calculation is 20% (error) of 70 = 14 servings.
Answer C is wrong. The kitchen should NOT prepare enough to have 18 servings of pastrami and kraut. The calculation is 25% (error) of 70 = 18 servings.
Answer D is wrong. The kitchen should NOT prepare enough to have 21 servings of pastrami and kraut. The calculation is 30% (error) of 70 = 21 servings.

Question #22
Answer A is wrong. Kim's productivity is $100 per hour.
Answer B is wrong. Roberto's productivity is $116.66 per hour.
Answer C is correct. Jamal's productivity is $131.25 per hour.
Answer D is wrong. Melee's productivity is $120 per hour.

Question #23
Answer A is correct. The calculation for the extended cost of these inventory items on hand is as follows:
1. 3 bushels × $20.00 per bushel = $60.00
2. 4 gallons × $2.00 per gallon = $8.00
3. ½ case × $35.00 per case = $17.50
4. $60.00 + $8.00 + $17.50 = $85.50

Answer B is wrong. A bad calculation mixed up the numbers as follows:
1. 4 bushels (error) × $20.00 per bushel = $80.00
2. 3 gallons (error) × $2.00 per gallon = $6.00
3. ½ case × $35.00 per case = $17.50
4. $80.00 + $6.00 + $17.50 = $103.50

Answer C is wrong. A bad calculation mixed up the numbers as follows:
1. 3 bushels × $35.00 (error) per bushel = $105.00
2. 4 gallons × $2.00 per gallon = $8.00
3. ½ case × $20.00 (error) per case = $10.00
4. $105.00+ $8.00 + $10.00= $123.00

Answer D is wrong. A bad calculation mixed up the numbers as follows:
1. ½ bushel (error) × $20.00 per bushel = $10.00
2. 3 gallons (error) × $2.00 per gallon = $6.00
3. 4 case (error) × $35.00 per case = $140.00
4. $10.00 + $6.00 + $140.00 = $156.50

Question #24
Answer A is wrong. Inventory costs and spoilage costs are components of food costs, one of the prime costs.
Answer B is wrong. Taxes and social security are examples of noncontrollable costs.
Answer C is correct. Food costs and labor costs are called prime costs, because they are the two largest controllable costs.
Answer D is wrong. Rent and licensing fees are fixed costs once they have been negotiated.

Question #25
Answer A is wrong. Customer expectations impact the markup differentiations and menu item categories for the price-value relationship. This has nothing to do with the menu product mix.
Answer B is wrong. Menu items' popularities and profit margins are added to the menu product mix analysis to perform a menu engineering analysis. Variances are the differences between the actual results and the standards.
Answer C is wrong. Standard recipe cards contain the recipe ingredients, the serving portions and the cooking instructions, NOT the menu product mix.
Answer D is correct. The menu product mix analyzes the quantities sold, the standard portion costs and the selling prices for each menu item to establish the composite food costs.

Question #26

Answer A is wrong. A 5% difference compares the difference in food costs with actual sales. 5,000/100,000 = 5%. The variance should compare the difference in food cost versus budgeted food costs or the difference in sales with budgeted sales.

Answer B is wrong. The food cost percentage is 25%, NOT the variance.

Answer C is correct. The calculation is as follows:
1. The actual food costs are $25,000.
   0.25 × $100,000 = $25,000
2. The variance is $5,000
   $30,000 – $25,000 = $5,000

Answer D is wrong. The actual food costs are $25,000, NOT the variance.
1. The actual food costs are $25,000.
   0.25 × $100,000 = $25,000
2. missed step (error)

Question #27

Answer A is wrong. This calculation uses the same value for cases on hand twice to derive a bad answer. (18 – 10 = 8; then 10 – 8 = 2) (error)

Answer B is correct. The calculation is as follows: 18 cases – 10 cases = 8 cases

Answer C is wrong. This calculation ignores the fact that there are 10 cases on hand.

Answer D is wrong. This calculation added the cases on hand to the par stock level. The calculation should be a subtraction.

Question #28

Answer A is wrong. This calculation transposes some digits in the benefits cost.
1. $68,000 – $21,600 (error) = $46,400.
2. $46,400 – $26,400 = $20,000

Answer B is correct. The calculation is as follows:
1. The remaining payroll available is $45,400.
   $68,000 – $12,600 = $55,400
2. The dollars available for variable-cost employees is $19,000.
   $55,400 – $26,400 = $29,000

Answer C is wrong. This calculation omits the cost of employee benefits.

$68,000 – $26,400 = $31,600 (error)

Answer D is wrong. This calculation omits the cost managers' salaries.

$68,000 – $12,600 = $55,400 (error)

Question #29

Answer A is correct. Standardized recipes are the management's control over ingredients, quantities, instructions, and portion sizes.

Answer B is wrong. Inventories represent the quantities and value of ingredients in storage. They do NOT include portion sizes or instructions.

Answer C is wrong. Food costs include the value of ingredients. The instructions and the portion sizes are NOT part of food costs.

Answer D is wrong. Corrective actions may or may NOT impact details about ingredients, quantities, instructions, and portion sizes.

Question #30

Answer A is wrong. This answer is the result of an incorrect calculation. $1000 × 0.25 = $250 (error) is NOT the weekly sales.

Answer B is wrong. $1000 is the weekly cost of food sold, NOT the sales.

Answer C is correct. The calculation of the actual sales is as follows: $1000 ÷ 0.25 = $4,000.

Answer D is wrong. For this answer to be correct, the food cost percentage would have to be 8%, NOT 25 %.

Question #31

Answer A is wrong. The calculation is as follows:
1. The average inventory for the month is $13,000.
   (15,000 + 11,000) ÷ 2 = $13,000
2. The turnover is NOT 0.2, which mixes up the numerator (cost of food sold) and the denominator (average inventory)
   $13,000 ÷ $ 65,000 = 0.2 (error)

Answer B is wrong. The calculation is an average *inventory* only and does NOT include the cost of food sold.
1. ($15,000 + $11,000 + $65,000) ÷ 3 = $30,333.00 (error)
2. The turnover is 2.14
   $65,000 ÷ $30,333 = 2.14

Answer C is correct. The calculation is as follows:
1. The average inventory for the month is $13,000.
   $(15,000 + 11,000) \div 2 = \$13,000$
2. The turnover is 5.0
   $\$65,000 \div \$13,000 = 5.0$

Answer D is wrong. The calculations are bad:
1. The calculation is an average and NOT the total of the inventory values and cost of food sold.
   $(\$15,000 + \$11,000 + \$65,000) = \$91,000$ (error)
2. The turnover is 5.0
   $\$91,000 \div \$13,000 = 7.0$

Question #32
Answer A is wrong. The usable amount is part of the definition of the edible portion (EP) costing method.
Answer B is wrong. The taste of ingredients has no impact on how ingredients are costed.
Answer C is correct. The AP portions are costed as they are received from suppliers.
Answer D is wrong. The AP method includes waste and shrinkage. The edible portion (EP) omits waste and shrinkage.

Question #33
Answer A is wrong. A variable cost changes in direct proportion to sales, not inventory.
Answer B is wrong. A variable cost changes in direct proportion to sales, not labor.
Answer C is wrong. A variable cost changes in direct proportion to sales, not profits.
Answer D is correct. A variable cost changes in direct proportion to sales.

Question #34

Answer A is wrong. Standing orders are typically used for specific products like bakery, coffee, or dairy products in various restaurant operations.

Answer B is wrong. Chain operations typically use the cost-plus purchasing.

Answer C is correct. Since schools, hospitals and the government cafeterias typically buy food supplies based on annual budget, they use the sealed bids method to bid on the total annual supplies.

Answer D is wrong. Chain operations or franchises typically use the commissary method from a centralized internal department.

Question #35

Answer A is wrong. Noncontrollable costs are NOT easy to control by definition. Managers have to budget the noncontrollable costs like rent, licenses, and insurance. Scheduling in controllable.

Answer B is wrong. The schedule does not impact fixed costs, those costs that are NOT proportional to sales.

Answer C is correct. The portion of labor costs that are variable (like hourly wages) are controlled with the work schedule.

Answer D is wrong. The work schedule can be used for staff discipline; however, that is NOT the primary purpose of the control tool.

Question #36

Answer A is wrong. For the food cost percentage to be 22%, the sale price would have to be $25.45 for food cost of $5.60; or the food cost would have to be $4.40 to sell at $20.00.

Answer B is wrong. For the food cost percentage to be 25%, the sale price would have to be $22.40 for food cost of $5.60; or the food cost would be $5.00 to sell at $20.00.

Answer C is correct. The calculation is food cost percentage = (cost ÷ sale price) × 100, or ($5.60 ÷ $20.00 = 0.28) x100 = 28 %.

Answer D is wrong. For the food cost percentage to be 30%, the sale price would have to be $18.67 for food cost of $5.60;.or the food cost would have to be $6.00 to sell at $20.00.

Question #37

Answer A is wrong. A fixed cost remains the same regardless of sales. This lease has a variable cost component that changes with sales.

Answer B is correct. This lease has a fixed cost component plus a variable cost component, so it is a semivariable cost.

Answer C is wrong. A variable cost changes in direct proportion to sales. This lease has a fixed cost component so it is not a variable cost.

Answer D is wrong. A manager cannot control the terms after the lease has been negotiated. So the lease is a noncontrollable cost.

Question #38

Answer A is correct. One person in charge brings the current stock up to par at the start of each shift. This action reduces the opportunities for theft because stock is traceable.

Answer B is wrong. Stock close to staff improves efficiency but NOT security.

Answer C is wrong. Inventories are not usually performed to prevent theft. The inventory can discover theft after the fact.

Answer D is wrong. Fewer items mean less potential theft. However there is a greater risk that the operations may run out of stock and hurt business.

Question #39

Answer A is correct. The items' margins and the items' popularity help the manager identify which items are (profitable and popular) or (unprofitable and popular) or (profitable and unpopular) or (unprofitable and unpopular). Menu engineering focuses the manager's attention on menu items that maximize profitability.

Answer B is wrong. The price-value relationship is an estimate of the customers' perception of the menu versus the competitors' menus, is NOT part of menu engineering.

Answer C is wrong. The markup differentiations categorize menu items into groups with similar markups. This activity does not account for the popularity of menu items that is part of menu engineering.

Answer D is wrong. Each menu item markup includes enough revenues to cover the labor and other expenses in the selling price. These numbers are included in the menu product mix, NOT added to the menu product mix.

Question #40
Answer A is wrong. With the figures given in this question, there is a decimal point error in this calculation.

Answer B is wrong. With the figures given in this question, the calculation does NOT use division. The calculation uses multiplication.

Answer C is correct. The calculation of the actual food cost is:

$$0.40 \times \$35,000 = \$14,000$$

Answer D is wrong. This value, $21,000, is the gross profit, which is calculated as follows:

$$\$35,000 - (0.40 \times \$35,000 = \$14,000) = \$21,000$$

Question #41
Answer A is wrong. $150 is too low. The projects indicate a rising trend, so a projection greater than $275 is better, unless there are external factors not described in the question.

Answer B is wrong. $200 is too low. The projects indicate a rising trend, so a projection greater than $275 is better, unless there are external factors not described in the question.

Answer C is correct. $300 is a reasonable projection. The projects indicate a rising trend, so a projection greater than $275 is better, unless there are external factors not described in the question.

Answer D is wrong. $375 is too high. The projections indicate a rising trend, but $375 seems too big a change to expect, unless there are external factors not described in the question.

Question #42
Answer A is wrong. ($18,000 + $10,500 (error) = $28,500) – $27,200 = $1,300 is an incorrect calculation. The correct formula is (opening inventory + purchases) – closing inventory = food costs.

Answer B is wrong. $27,200 is only the food purchases. The correct formula is (opening inventory + purchases) – closing inventory = food costs.

Answer C is correct. ($18,000 + $27,200 = $45,200) – $10,500 = $34,700 is the correct calculation. The correct formula is (opening inventory + purchases) – closing inventory = food costs.

Answer D is wrong. $18,000 + $10,500 + $27,200 (error) = $55,700 is an incorrect calculation. The correct formula is (opening inventory + purchases) – closing inventory = food costs.

Question #43

Answer A is wrong. The manager decides whether the effort to preportion food is worth scheduling extra hours, which increases labor costs.

Answer B is correct. Efficient and accurate portion control is a good mechanism to control food costs.

Answer C is wrong. The staff must still prepare the food for customer orders. Preportioning simplifies some of the tasks during preparation but does not enable taking breaks during food prep time.

Answer D is wrong. Preportioning just shifts the portioning effort to a different time and can make the work more efficient. Preportioning does NOT eliminate the task of portioning or eliminate any other program.

Question #44

Answer A is wrong. Health insurance, dental insurance, worker's compensation insurance and social security (FICA) taxes are part of the employee benefits package. Employee benefits are only part of the total labor costs.

Answer B is wrong. Wages and salaries are two types of payroll expenses. Payroll is only part of the total labor costs

Answer C is wrong. It is true that total labor costs are usually considered semivariable. For example salaries are considered fixed costs while wages are considered variable costs. However, total labor costs are NEVER categorized as a fixed cost.

Answer D is correct. The payroll costs plus the costs for employee benefits is the total labor costs as expressed on an income statement.

Question #45

Answer A is correct. Using the oldest items first helps to reduce spoilage in storage.

Answer B is wrong. Using the oldest item last is last in/first out (LIFO) stock rotation.

Answer C is wrong. Using the newest item first is last in/first out (LIFO) stock rotation.

Answer D is wrong. Placing dates on the stock, by itself, does not ensure that the staff rotates the stock.

Question #46
Answer A is wrong. The conversion factor is a multiplying factor, NOT a dividing factor.

12 ounces $\div$ 1.2 = 10 ounces (error)

Answer B is wrong. The conversion factor is a multiplying factor, NOT an addition factor.

12 ounces + 1.2 = 13.2 ounces (error)

Answer C is correct. The calculation is as follows:

12 ounces $\times$ 1.2 = 14.4 ounces.

Answer D is wrong. 19.2 ounces of light cream is required, NOT 19.2 ounces of crab meat.

16 ounces $\times$ 1.2 = 19.6 ounces. (error)

Question 47
Answer A is wrong. The invoice only reflects supplies that have been received. The receiver should match the salmon specifications to the purchase order.

Answer B is wrong. The standard recipe identifies the general name of the ingredients. The specification details all the product characteristics.

Answer C is wrong. The par stock deals only with the quantity of products in inventory, NOT the characteristics of the products.

Answer D is correct. The specification ties the menu item description and quality to the purchase of the salmon supplies.

Question #48
Answer A is wrong. These numbers indicate that the yield was not factored into the calculations.

Answer B is wrong. These numbers did not calculate the servings per unit (SPUs) correctly.

Answer C is wrong. The amount of fish and chicken is reversed.

Answer D is correct. The calculations are as follows:

Fish calculation:
1. The SPU is 1.6 servings per unit (SPUs).
    16 oz $\div$ 10 oz = 1.6 SPUs;
2. The PF is 0.8 purchase factor (PF)
    1.6 SPUs $\times$ 50% yield = 0.8 purchase factor (PF);
3. The buyer orders 150 pounds of fish
    200 servings $\div$ 0.8 PF = 150 pounds of fish

Chicken calculation:
1. The SPU is 2 servings per unit (SPUs).
   16 oz ÷ 8 oz = 2 SPUs;
2. The PF is 1.5 purchase factor (PF)
   2 SPUs × 75% yield = 1.5 PF;
3. The buyer orders 200 pounds of chicken
   300 servings ÷ 1.5 PF = 200 pounds of chicken

Question #49

Answer A is correct. Opening inventory plus purchases is the total food available. Then the total food available minus the closing inventory gives the actual cost of food sold for the reporting period. The closing inventory is available food, carried over to the next reporting period as opening inventory.

Answer B is wrong. The closing inventory must NOT be added because this is NOT a cost of food sold.

Answer C is wrong. Purchases CANNOT be subtracted from the opening inventory because purchases are new costs of available food. The closing inventory must not be added because this is NOT a cost of food sold.

Answer D is wrong. Purchases CANNOT be subtracted from the opening inventory because purchases are new costs of available food.

Question #50

Answer A is wrong. The perpetual inventory is used track inventory for different units of the same operation.

Answer B is correct. The physical inventory tracks the actual supplies on hand for calculating food costs.

Answer C is wrong. The perpetual inventory value is used to estimate the daily food cost percentage.

Answer D is wrong. The FIFO stock rotation helps control spoilage.

Controlling Foodservice Costs Glossary

Actual price method   inventory valuation method that uses the actual price paid for the product to compute closing inventory values

As purchased (AP) method   used to cost an ingredient at the purchase price prior to considering any trim or waste

As served (AS)   amount available to serve to the customer

Averaged price method   inventory valuation method that uses a composite of all prices paid for an item during the inventory period to value the closing inventory

Bank   specific amount of coins and currency sufficient to make change for guests

Budget   projection of sales, costs, and profit that is used to guide day-to-day operational decisions

Butcher test   process in which a wholesale cut of meat is broken down into a retail cut and the trim, bone, and waste are analyzed and recorded to arrive at an EP cost for the retail cut; also used to measure the amount of shrinkage that occurs during the trimming of meat products

Buyer   person who purchases products for the restaurant

Cash handling procedure   activities followed to ensure that all cash and charge transactions are accurate and accounted for

Cash report   form filled out by cashiers to report all money, checks, and charge slips collected during a shift

Closing inventory   inventory value at the end of an accounting period

Commissary purchasing method used by chains and franchised units; orders from individual units are consolidated, and the commissary purchases the total quantity needed from preferred suppliers

Competitive quotes purchasing method in which the buyer gives suppliers a market quotation sheet indicating items and applicable quantities to be purchased; suppliers then provide a price quote for the items

Composite food cost percentage weighted average food cost percentage for all items sold; also called weighted food cost percentage

Control method of exercising some amount of power over events or situations to achieve a particular result

Controllable cost cost that management can directly control

Conversion chart list of food items showing the expected, or average, shrinkage from AP amount to EP amount

Conversion factor multiplier used to increase or decrease quantities in a standardized recipe

Cooking loss test way to measure the amount of product shrinkage during the cooking or roasting process

Corrective action steps to correct a problem when there are variances between budget plans and actual operating results

Cost of food sold dollar amount spent on food; calculation: opening inventory plus purchases, minus the ending inventory

Cost plus purchasing method in which a restaurant's purchases are invoiced at the supplier's cost plus an agreed-upon markup

Covers per server number of customer meals that a server can serve in one hour

Credit card   form of payment that obligates users to pay the credit card company for the products and services charged to the card

Crew schedule   chart that shows employees' names and the days and times they are to work

Daily food cost   estimate of food cost based upon requisitions, transfers, and sales

Daily sales report   form that shows sales, cash, and charges collected, as well as any shift overages or shortages

Debit card   form of payment by which the amount charged is immediately withdrawn from the cardholder's bank account

Duplicate guest-check system   control procedure that uses a two-copy written record of guests' purchases and charges

Edible portion (EP) method   used to cost an ingredient after it has been trimmed and waste has been removed so that only the usable portion of the item is considered

Employee benefits   valuable, nonwage compensation provided to employees by employers

Employee turnover   number of employees hired to fill one position in one year's time

Extending   multiplying the number of units of a stored item by that item's unit price

Factor method   used to determine a menu item's sales price based simply on the basis of the standard food cost percentage

Federal Insurance Contributions Act (FICA)   program for retirement and medical benefits administered by the Federal government and paid for by employers and employees

FIFO method   first in, first out; inventory valuation method that uses the latest price paid for an item to value inventory and that requires older products be utilized before newer products

Fixed cost   cost that remains the same regardless of sales volume

Food cost   actual dollar value of the food used by an operation during a certain period

Food cost percentage   relationship between sales and the cost spent on food to achieve those sales

Food production chart   form that details how much product is to be produced by the kitchen during a specified time period

Gross profit   amount of money made after the cost of food sold is subtracted from food sales

Income statement   report showing sales, costs, and the profit or loss of a business

Inventory   itemized list of goods and products, their on-hand quantity, and their total dollar value

Inventory breakdown   method of categorizing an operation's food and supplies

Inventory turnover   measure of how frequently the total value of stored items has been turned (replaced) during a specific accounting period

Invoice   a bill that accompanies the delivery of goods

Issuing   removing food or beverage products from storage

Job description   statement that details an employee's duties and the standards to which he or she is expected to perform those duties

Labor contract   agreement between management and a union that represents the employees and deals with information about wages, employee benefits, hours, and working conditions

Labor cost   includes, in addition to payroll cost, such costs as the employer's contribution to FICA and Medicare, worker's compensation insurance, and all employee benefits

Labor cost percent   ratio of labor cost and business volume (labor cost divided by sales volume equals labor cost percent)

Labor expense   the payroll for hourly employees and salaried management; also includes FICA and Medicare payments and employee benefit costs

Latest price method   also known as FIFO; inventory valuation method that uses the latest price paid for a product to value inventory

LIFO method   last in, first out; inventory valuation method that uses the price paid for the oldest product to value inventory and that requires the newest products to be utilized before older products

Line item review   a comparison of all budgeted items against operating results with differences noted

Loss   when expenses are greater than sales

Market quotation sheet   standardized form that is given to two or more suppliers who are then asked to provide a price quote for the items needed

Markup   the difference between the actual (food) cost of producing an item and its selling price listed on the menu

Markup differentiation   relationship between cost of an item and its price after markup

Markup on cost method   another method used to determine a menu item's selling price based on the standard food cost percentage

Master schedule   template, usually a spreadsheet, showing the number of people needed in each position to operate the restaurant

Medicare   money set aside for health benefits for those who cannot afford them

Menu engineering   menu evaluation process that considers the contribution margin and popularity of each menu item

Menu product mix   a detailed analysis that shows the quantities sold of each item, along with their selling prices and standard portion costs

Noncontrollable cost   cost over which management has little or no control
Nonperishable goods   products that have a relatively long shelf life

One-stop shop   purchasing method in which most, if not all, of an operation's products are purchased from one supplier

Opening inventory   value of inventory at the beginning of a given period

Overtime   any hours worked over forty in a work week

Padding   inappropriate activity of adding a dollar value for nonexistent inventory items to the dollar value of total inventory

Par stock   the level of inventory that must always be in stock in the restaurant

Payroll dollars   number of dollars available for payroll during a scheduling period

Perishable goods   products with a relatively short shelf life (usually one to three days)

Perpetual inventory   theoretical inventory count based on products received and issued
Person-hour   also referred to as labor hours; the total hours worked by hourly (variable-cost) employees for a given period of time

Physical inventory   actual physical count and valuation of all items on hand

Plate presentation   how an item will look to the guest when it is served

Point-of-sale (POS) control system   computerized cash and product sales management system

Portion control   ensuring the service of a proper portion as determined by the standardized recipe or the company standard

Portion control device   implement that assists with the proper portioning of food items
Portion size   size of a menu item

Preportioned item   food that is measured or weighed prior to being placed on the service line

Price-value relationship   connection between the selling price of an item and its worth to the customer

Prime costs   two highest costs in most operations food and labor

Productivity standard   level set by management to measure the quality and amount of work performed by an employee

Product usage report   form that shows the number of items issued to the cook's line, the number returned to inventory, and the number sold to guests

Profit   dollar amount remaining after all operational expenses are subtracted from sales

Pro forma income statement   income statement that is prepared before the fact

Purchase order   form listing products to be purchased, agreed-upon price, required delivery date, and other important information that a buyer sends to a supplier as confirmation for a purchase

Purchases   value of the food purchased during a specific period

Quality standard   level of excellence used to measure customer satisfaction

Quotes   prices cited by a supplier for a specific product

Recipe conversion   method used to change the yield of a recipe from its original yield to a desired yield

Recipe cost card   tool used to calculate standard portion cost for a menu item

Recipe yield   number of individual portions that a recipe will produce

Requisitions   forms that contain specifics about items to be issued from storage areas

Return chart   chart that is filled out to explain why a customer returned an item to the kitchen

Sales   dollar amount the restaurant has taken in from food purchased by customers

Sealed bid   prices provided by a supplier who does not have knowledge of the prices proposed by other bids because each bid is submitted in a "sealed envelope"

Semivariable cost   cost that increases and decreases as, respectively, sales increase and decrease, but not in direct proportion

Shrinkage   amount of loss incurred when a product is trimmed and cooked, roasted, or otherwise prepared for service

Specification   document listing the product name, its intended use, grade, size, and other product characteristics that represent the quality standard of the item as established by the buyer

Standard   measure established to compare levels of attainment for a goal or other measure of adequacy

Standardized recipe   lists the ingredients and quantities needed for a menu item, as well as the methods used to produce it and its portion size

Standard portion cost   exact amount that one serving or portion of a food item should cost when prepared according to the item's standardized recipe that has been pre-costed with current purchase cost

Standing order   purchasing method in which a par stock is established by the operation and then that level of inventory is maintained by the supplier

Taste test   product sampling performed prior to the start of a meal period to determine if products to be served meet the restaurant's standards

Texas Restaurant Association (TRA) markup method   menu price calculation method that reflects the direct relationship between profit and selling price

Time and temperature control   policies and procedures that monitor the time and temperatures of food that is held before service to guests

Total expense   includes labor, as well as all other controllable and noncontrollable expenses

Total food available   dollar amount of all food available for sale, computed as beginning inventory plus purchases
Transfer   process of moving products and their cost from one foodservice unit or department to another

Variable cost   cost that should increase and decrease in direct proportion to sales

Waste report   form used to track food that was deemed unfit for sale; it also indicates the cause of the food waste

Yield chart   listing of the EP weight of products (as opposed to their AP weight) and an average yield percentage

Yield percentage   the EP weight of a product divided by its AP weight

Yield test   analysis done to determine the difference between a product's AP weight and its EP weight